GREAT AMERICAN

HORSES

AN IMAGINATION LIBRARY SERIES

STANDARDBREDS

by Victor Gentle and Janet Perry

Gareth Stevens Publishing
A WORLD ALMANAC EDUCATION GROUP COMPANY

Thanks to Gary Spears, for all the standard reasons. And, inspired by Sharon McQueen, who always goes beyond the standard.

—Victor Gentle and Janet Perry

Please visit our web site at: www.garethstevens.com
For a free color catalog describing Gareth Stevens' list of high-quality books and
multimedia programs, call 1-800-542-2595 (USA) or 1-800-461-9120 (Canada).
Gareth Stevens Publishing's Fax: (414) 332-3567.

Library of Congress Cataloging-in-Publication Data

Gentle, Victor.
  Standardbreds / by Victor Gentle and Janet Perry.
    p. cm. — (Great American horses: an imagination library series)
  Includes bibliographical references (p. 23) and index.
  ISBN 0-8368-2939-5 (lib. bdg.)
  1. Standardbred horse—United States—Juvenile literature. [1. Standardbred horse.
  2. Horses.] I. Perry, Janet, 1960- II. Title.
  SF293.S72G46   2001
  636.1'75—dc21   2001020848

First published in 2001 by
Gareth Stevens Publishing
A World Almanac Education Group Company
330 West Olive Street, Suite 100
Milwaukee, WI 53212 USA

Text: Victor Gentle and Janet Perry
Page layout: Victor Gentle, Janet Perry, and Scott M. Krall
Cover design: Renee M. Bach
Series editor: Katherine J. Meitner
Picture researcher: Diane Laska-Swanke

Photo credits: Cover, pp. 5, 7, 15, 17, 21 Courtesy of the U.S. Trotting Association; pp. 9, 19, 22
© Bob Langrish; pp. 11, 13 Courtesy of the Harness Racing Museum and Hall of Fame, Goshen, New York

Printed in the United States of America

1 2 3 4 5 6 7 8 9 05 04 03 02 01

Front cover: This is Jet Laag as he sets a new world record in 1999 for **pacing** a mile in 1 minute 49 seconds (1:49)!

TABLE OF CONTENTS

Words that appear in the glossary are printed in **boldface** type the first time they occur in the text.

"THEY'RE OFF!"

The starting gates slap open! Hooves pound, leather snaps, wheels whir, nostrils flare, and legs blur. The horses speed past the stands. Their ears turn back for the slightest signal from their drivers. They breathe deeply, huffing and puffing and stretching their necks for the finish.

These horses are Standardbreds. They are **bred** especially to race. For hundreds of years, people carefully bred together the fastest **mares** and **stallions** around to produce even faster **foals**. It worked, because these horses are *fast!*

If they are bred to be the fastest, why are they called "standard"?

A close-up of a tight race. The horse closest to you is behind right now, but anything can happen at the races!

GAITED TO SET THE PACE

Before the American Revolution, colonists on the East Coast loved a good horse race. After the war, many land owners had two types of horses. They used "heavy" horses for hard work in fields and "light" horses for riding or pulling carriages.

Light horses were bred for racing because they had the right **gaits**. They could **pace**, **trot**, canter, and gallop. The canter is a slow run and the gallop is a fast run. Trotting and pacing are "in-between" gaits — not walking or running.

When a horse trots, its front leg and the opposite back leg step forward together. When it paces, its right legs go forward at the same time, followed by the left legs.

Sometimes Standardbreds race with a rider, a style of racing called "under saddle." The closest horse has straps on its legs to keep it from losing its gait.

SPEED, SPIRIT, AND GRACE

Smart landowners saved money by having horses that could do more than one thing. These horses could pull carriages, were easy to ride, and could trot or pace a mile at blazing speeds.

By 1879, horses had to be able to race a mile in the "standard" time of two and a half minutes in order to compete in any **harness** races. Horses that were bred to do that were called Standardbreds.

The best harness racing horses had Thoroughbred and saddle horse parents. Thoroughbreds gave the foals speed and spirit. Saddle horses gave the foals gaits and grace.

A fine Standardbred named White Tye, eating on the trot.

THAT WINNING PITCH

The first Standardbred **foundation sire** was born in 1849. His name was Hambletonian, named after an ancient horse race in England — the Hambleton. But he did not have a great start. His father was ugly and mean. His mother was lame.

His owner was sure he would fail. After all, Hambletonian was strangely built. His **withers** were lower than his rump! A horse's rump and withers, people thought, should be the same height.

William Rysdyk was the man who took care of Hambletonian. He was sure that this little horse was bound for glory. He bought Hambletonian and his mother for $125. Hambletonian was the father of the fastest foals around.

Hambletonian had what was called "trotter's pitch." The rump height meant that his hind legs were extra powerful for trotting.

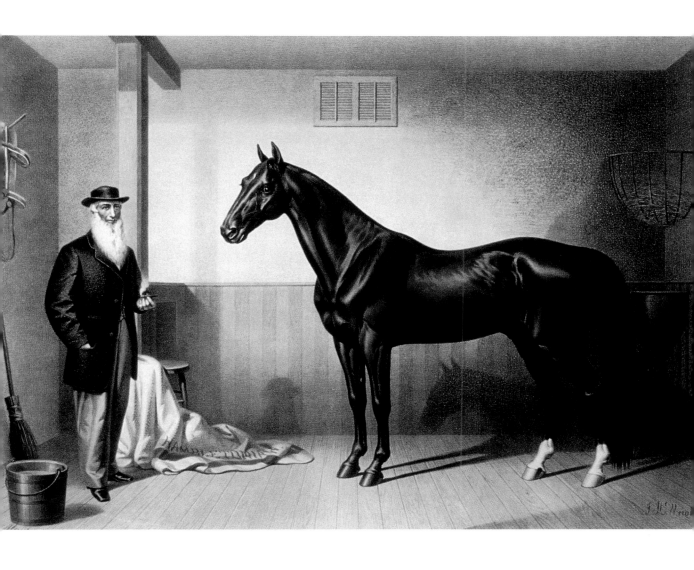

A HIGHER STANDARD

From 1902 to 1920, the most famous American celebrity was not a movie star or a baseball player. He was a Standardbred Horse named Dan Patch.

Dan himself was born with a twisted leg. His owner looked at him and thought he was not built to win. Yet from his first race to his last, Dan never lost. In one year, Dan Patch traveled across the country, paced in shows for huge audiences, and set five world records. In his life, he set nine world records and earned millions of dollars for his owner.

Toys, a train line, washing machines, and dance steps were named in honor of this lovable, breathtakingly fast racehorse.

The wheels behind Dan Patch had to be set 8 inches (20 centimeters) wider than normal because of the odd kick he gave with his twisted leg.

OTHERWORLDLY SPEED

He was a trotting horse with two names. Unlike most horses, his official name was one word — Greyhound. His long, scruffy body looked more like a skinny racing dog, not a fine horse. He finished first seventy-one times and broke twenty-five records in his life. To challenge him was like trying to catch a ghost. So his fans called him "Gray Ghost."

Americans needed heroes in the 1930s. Many people were hungry and out of work. They loved Greyhound, even when he lost. He was not perfect. People thought that if he could fight back and win, maybe they could, too. The Gray Ghost lifted their spirits.

Shoulder to tail, horses are about as long as they are high. Greyhound was 4 inches (10.2 cm) longer than he was tall.

"SILK IS BETTER THAN GOLD"

Silk Stockings was not big with bulging muscles. She was a strong pacer with long legs. To Ken and Claire Mazik, Silky looked too dainty to win races. But Silky was the horse they could afford.

When the Maziks bought Silky, they hoped she would win enough race money to help pay for their school for autistic children. Autistic kids have trouble understanding the world around them. Silky broke through. She helped the kids feel good about the world outside. They wanted her to win and cheered for her when she did.

Silky set seven world records for pacing and gave the Maziks' kids a lot to believe in. Silky was truly worth more than the money she won.

Silky set a record time of 1:57.3 at Monticello, New York. Here she is, the golden girl, setting the pace.

STANDARD USES

Hambletonian, Dan Patch, Greyhound, and Silk Stockings were all winning Standardbred Horses. They were also very different from each other in size and shape. Hambletonian was built strong and stocky. Dan Patch had a twisted leg. Greyhound was long and big. Silk Stockings was slender. So what, exactly, makes a horse a Standardbred?

If a foal is born with Standardbred parents, it is also a Standardbred. Standardbreds have been carefully bred with many different qualities. So even if they are not very good at racing, they are still good at other things.

This foal is a Standardbred. If it cannot make record times at the track, it may have other winning talents that a good trainer will find.

ADOPTING GOOD STANDARDS

Standardbred Horses are also good riding, jumping, and harness horses. Standardbreds will often race for only two to ten years. Most of their lives they are not racing. Horses can live up to thirty years, if they are well cared for.

People can adopt Standardbreds that no longer race. Adopted horses are great at being trail horses, competing in riding, jumping, or wagon driving competitions, or as horses that help disabled riders get some exercise. Standardbreds are great horses for a lot of different uses; they hold a high standard of excellence in everything they do.

Moni Maker won Horse of the Year in 1998 and 1999. Here she is in 2000 with a new record of 1:54. She had heart trouble, but she never quit.

DIAGRAM AND SCALE OF A HORSE

Here's how to measure a horse with a show of hands.
See how this Standardbred is taller at the croup than
the withers? There is that winning "trotter's pitch"!

Ear

Crest

Poll

Mane

Forelock

Neck

Withers

Face

Croup

Back

Hip

Dock

Nostril

Cheek

Tail

Shoulder

Chest

Thigh

Elbow

Gaskin

Barrel

Knee

Hock

Cannon

Ankle

Hoof

6 ft. (180 cm) — 18 hh, 17 hh, 16 hh, 15 hh
5 ft. (150 cm) — 15 hh, 14 hh, 13 hh
4 ft. (120 cm) — 13 hh, 12 hh, 11 hh
3 ft. (90 cm) — 10 hh, 9 hh
2 ft. (60 cm) — 8 hh, 7 hh, 6 hh, 5 hh
1 ft. (30 cm) — 4 hh, 3 hh, 2 hh
1 hand

(10-year-old)

1 hand high (hh) = 4 inches (approximately 10 cm)

WHERE TO WRITE OR CALL FOR MORE INFORMATION

United States Trotting Association
750 Michigan Avenue
Columbus, OH 43215-1191
Phone: (614) 224-2291

22

MORE TO READ AND VIEW

Books (Fiction):   *Classic Horse and Pony Stories*. Edited by Diana Pullein-Thompson (Dorling Kindersley)

Books (Nonfiction):   *Born to Trot*. Marguerite Henry (Aladdin)
The Complete Guides to Horses and Ponies (series). Jackie Budd (Gareth Stevens)
DK Riding Club: Horse and Pony Breeds. Carolyn Henderson (Dorling Kindersley)
Great American Horses (series). Victor Gentle and Janet Perry (Gareth Stevens)
United States Pony Club Manual of Horsemanship: Basics for Beginners. Susan E. Harris (Hungry Minds)

Magazines: *Horse Illustrated* and its new magazine for young readers, *Young Rider*

Videos (Nonfiction):   *Noble Horse*. (National Geographic)
The Real Cowboy: Portrait of an American Icon. (Discovery Communications)
Ultimate Guide to Horses. (Discovery Channel)

WEB SITES

The United States Trotting Association
www.ustrotting.com

For more information on Standardbreds:
www.hhyf.org

For general horse information:
www.henry.k12.ga.us/pges/kid-pages/
horse-mania/index.htm
horsefun.com/facts/factfldr/facts.html

Some web sites stay current longer than others. To find additional web sites, use a reliable search engine, such as Yahooligans or KidsClick! (http://sunsite.berkeley.edu/KidsClick!/), with one or more of the following key words to help you locate information about horses: *Dan Patch, Hambletonian, harness racing, Standardbred Horses,* and *trotting*.

GLOSSARY

You can find these words on the pages listed. Reading a word in a sentence helps you understand it even better.

bred (past tense of breed)(v) — to have chosen a stallion and a mare with certain features as a result of the careful selection of stallions and mares to mate 4, 6, 8, 18

foal (FOHL) — a baby horse 4, 8, 10, 18

foundation sire — a male horse, or one of the male horses, from which all horses in a breed must be descended 10

gait — a way of moving. Walking, running, pacing, trotting, and cantering are examples of horse gaits 6, 8

harness (HARR-ness) — straps of leather or rope that wrap around a horse's body and attach to a wagon, cart, coach, or buggy so that the horse can pull it 8, 20

mare — an adult female horse 4

pace — to use a gait with two beats, where the legs move together, first on one side and then the other 2, 6, 8, 12, 16

stallion — an adult male horse 4

trot — a gait with two beats, where diagonally opposite legs hit the ground at the same time 6, 8, 10, 14

withers (WITH-urz) — the ridge between the shoulder bones of a horse. Horses' heights are measured to the withers 10

INDEX